W9-AXZ-093

TONI
MORRISON

—African-American Biographies—

TONI MORRISON
Nobel Prize-Winning Author

Series Consultant:
Dr. Russell L. Adams, Chairman
Department of Afro-American Studies, Howard University

Barbara Kramer

Enslow Publishers, Inc.

44 Fadem Road	PO Box 38
Box 699	Aldershot
Springfield, NJ 07081	Hants GU12 6BP
USA	UK

Library of Congress Cataloging-in-Publication Data

Kramer, Barbara.
    Toni Morrison, Nobel Prize-winning author / Barbara Kramer.
        p. cm. — (African-American biographies)
    Includes bibliographical references and index.
    Summary: Examines the life and work of the successful novelist, who
became the first African American to win the Nobel Prize in Literature in
1993.
        ISBN 0-89490-688-7
        1. Morrison, Toni—Biography—Juvenile literature. 2. Afro-American
women novelists—20th century—Biography—Juvenile literature.
[1. Morrison, Toni. 2. Authors, American. 3. Afro-Americans—Biography.
4. Women—Biography.] I.Title. II. Series.
PS3563.08749Z74   1996
813'.54—dc20
    [B]   96-752
                                                                                     CIP
                                                                                      AC
Printed in the United States of America

10 9 8 7 6 5 4 3 2 1

Illustration Credits: AP/Wide World Photos, p. 91; Bernard
Gotfryd/Woodfin Camp, pp. 36, 43, 71; Black River Historical Society,
p. 19; Ed Geller/Globe Photos, Inc., 1995, p. 95; ©1978 Helen Marcus,
p. 51; Imapress/Globe Photos, Inc., p. 6; Joe Pineiro, University
Photographer, Columbia University, p. 79; © Kate Kunz, p. 85; Laura
Pedrick/The New York Times, pp. 9, 83; Moorland-Spingarn Research
Center, Howard University Archives, pp. 23, 24, 26; Photo by Jim
Kolaczko, provided courtesy of the Lorain Public Library System, p. 94;
University Archives, State University of New York at Albany, pp. 64, 66.

Cover Illustration: AP/Wide World Photos

CONTENTS

1 Excitement on Campus 7

2 Stories, Ghosts, and Dreams 12

3 An Unanswered Prayer 21

4 *The Bluest Eye* 30

5 Friendship and Evil 39

6 A Career Takes Flight 46

7 Politics and Race 56

8 "Sixty Million and More" 69

9 That "Dirty, Get-on-Down Music" 81

10 Writing for Life 93

Chronology 98

Chapter Notes 100

Further Reading 109

Index 110

Toni Morrison

1

EXCITEMENT ON CAMPUS

There was excitement on the Princeton University campus. It was October 7, 1993, and an important announcement had just been made. Toni Morrison, one of Princeton's own faculty members, had been selected to receive the world's highest honor for a writer—the Nobel Prize in literature. Reporters were on campus hoping to get a statement from Morrison. Nevertheless, for Morrison, it was business as usual. The reporters had to wait until she was finished teaching her literature class.

Morrison had started her day at 4:30 A.M. when she got up to write. She was startled when the phone rang about 7:00 A.M. "I knew it was terrible news," Morrison remembers. "And when a friend of mine on the other end said, 'Did you hear?' then I knew it was something awful."[1]

It turned out to be just the opposite. Her friend had already learned that Morrison was to be awarded the 1993 Nobel Prize in literature, and she was calling to congratulate Morrison.

Later that day Morrison received an official call from the secretary of the Swedish Academy confirming that she was indeed the winner. She still had trouble believing the news. The secretary told her a letter was on the way. "I said, 'Why don't you send me a fax?'" Morrison recalled. "Somehow, I felt that if I saw a fax, I'd know it wasn't a dream or somebody's hallucination."[2]

The award is named for its founder, Alfred Nobel, a Swedish scientist. Awards are given annually in the categories of physics, chemistry, medicine or physiology, literature, and peace. Morrison was the first African American to win in the area of literature. In a statement released through her publisher, she said, "Winning as an American is very special—but winning as a black American is a knockout."[3]

Two months later she traveled to Stockholm, Sweden, to receive the award. She arrived on Monday, December 6, after flying through the night. Winter days are short in that northern country. The sun had

Toni Morrison talks to reporters on the Princeton University campus after learning that she will be awarded the 1993 Nobel Prize in literature.

risen at 8:45 A.M. and had already set by 3:00 P.M., but there was hardly time to notice the lack of sunlight. Organizers for the Nobel Prize committee had planned a week's worth of events, including dinners, concerts, and press conferences.

On Tuesday, Morrison had lunch at the American Embassy. That afternoon there was a police escort to take her to the Swedish Academy where she was to give her Nobel lecture. Morrison wore a black gown for the occasion. It had sequins that reflected light from the thirteen chandeliers that decorated the hall.

She began her lecture with the words generations of children have grown up hearing: "Once upon a time . . ."[4] She spoke slowly, rhythmically, telling a story about a woman who was both blind and wise.

As she spoke, there was a curious rustling noise coming from the audience of about four hundred people. It was the shuffling of paper. Copies of Morrison's lecture had been handed out in advance. Some of the people in the audience were reading along with Morrison as she talked, not wanting to miss a single word. Morrison spoke for half an hour and then was rewarded with a standing ovation.

The actual presentation of the award took place on Friday evening. The festivities began with a trumpet fanfare and a procession led by Toni Morrison, who was escorted by the king of Sweden.

In 1993, the Nobel Prize in literature had a

monetary value of $825,000. Reporters asked Morrison what she would do with the money, but she said she did not know. "This is new to me, having to decide what to do with money," she joked. "I have no history of having to make such decisions."[5]

Morrison had made her mark in the world of literature as an editor, a teacher, and a writer. Her first novel, *The Bluest Eye*, told the story of an African-American girl who prayed every night for blue eyes. She associated blue eyes with beauty. The book was published in 1970. Five other novels followed, including *Sula*; *Song of Solomon*; *Tar Baby*; *Beloved*, which won the Pulitzer Prize in 1988; and *Jazz*, published in 1992.

As a child, Morrison had never dreamed of being a writer. She wanted to be a dancer like Maria Tallchief, a Native American ballerina. She began writing when she was an adult. With the publication of her first novel, Morrison knew that writing was something she would never give up. "I wasn't able to stop," she said. "It [writing] was for me the most extraordinary way of thinking and feeling—it became the one thing I was doing that I had absolutely no intention of living without."[6]

2

STORIES, GHOSTS, AND DREAMS

oni Morrison was born in Lorain, Ohio, on February 18, 1931. She was the second oldest of four children born to George and Ramah Wofford. They named her Chloe Anthony Wofford.

Although Chloe was born in Ohio, she had southern roots. Her mother's family was from Alabama. They had moved north in the early 1900s looking for a better way of life. Chloe's father, George Wofford, was originally from Georgia. He moved north when he was sixteen years old, hoping to escape the racism of the South.

Chloe was born when the United States was in the

midst of the Great Depression and unemployment was high. Her father worked anywhere jobs were available, sometimes holding down as many as three jobs simultaneously to provide for his family. At various times, he had been a car washer, a road construction worker, a steel mill welder, and a welder in the shipyards.

He took pride in his work. He once told Chloe that whenever he welded a perfect seam on a ship, he signed his name to it. "No one else saw it, or really even cared," Morrison later said. "But *he* cared, and that is all that mattered."[1]

In spite of his hard work, he was sometimes unemployed. During one of those times, when Chloe was only two years old, her parents could not come up with the $4 for their monthly rent. The landlord asked them to leave, but George Wofford refused. The landlord then set fire to the house with Chloe, her parents, and her older sister inside. Fortunately, no one was injured.

Chloe was too young to remember the fire, but her parents told her that story many times as she was growing up. In a strange way, Morrison says the story taught her about the importance of having a sense of humor. She says it was the only way to handle that kind of evil. Thinking about how little their lives were worth to the landlord was depressing, so instead, she laughed. "That's what laughter does," Morrison says. "You take it back. You take your life back."[2]

Chloe's mother, Ramah Wofford, was a strong-willed woman who believed in speaking out against injustice. Morrison remembers:

> My mother, when she would find out that they were not letting Black people sit in certain sections of the local theater, would go and sit in the white folks' section, go see *Superman* just so she could come out and say, "I sat there, so everybody else can too." [3]

Once during the Depression when the family received free flour from the government, they found it was infested with bugs. Ramah Wofford took her complaints straight to the top by writing a letter to President Franklin Roosevelt himself. "My mother believed something should be done about inhuman situations," Morrison said.[4]

Although times were hard, Chloe's childhood was not bleak. The Wofford home was filled with music. Ramah Wofford was in the church choir, and she was always singing around the house—jazz, blues, gospel music, and opera. Chloe's grandfather, John Solomon Willis, played the violin and for a while had supported his family with his music.

Storytelling was an important part of the family's entertainment. Morrison remembered her parents telling wonderful ghost stories. "My father's were the best," she said, "the scariest. We were always begging him to repeat the stories that terrified us the most."[5]

Reading was also a source of pleasure. Chloe's

mother belonged to a book club even though the family did not have much money. She taught Chloe that books were to be treasured. Chloe's grandfather had only gone to school one day in his life, and that was just to tell the teacher that he would not be back. "Yet all of his adult life he read greedily, as did his uneducated friends," Morrison later wrote.[6] Chloe learned to read at an early age and was the only child in her first grade class who could already read at the beginning of the school year.

The Woffords lived in an integrated neighborhood, and Chloe went to school with German, Irish, Italian, Greek, and African-American children. "People in small Midwestern towns came from everywhere," Morrison explained.[7] Even so, there were religious and ethnic lines that people did not cross. African Americans were barred from some places in town, such as the lake in the city park where white children went to swim.

Morrison also remembers racial slurs from other white boys who threw rocks at her and her friends and called them names. "Even then, I thought, 'How weak they must be—fourteen-year-old boys, attacking six-year-old girls half their size,'" Morrison said.[8] Although she had a mature attitude about their name-calling, it did not stop her fear—". . . their rocks *connected!* . . ." she remembers.[9]

School was one of two types of education in Chloe's

life. The other was the African-American cultural education that she got from her parents and grandparents. They taught her about African-American folklore, myths, and signs and visitations.

The supernatural had a place in their everyday lives. "I grew up in a house in which people talked about their dreams with the same authority that they talked about what 'really' happened," Morrison recalled.[10]

Her grandmother had a book to interpret dreams, and she used it to play the numbers. She would ask Chloe about her dreams, and then she referred to her book, which translated the dreams to a three-digit number. Chloe's grandmother won with Chloe's dreams for a while, but when she stopped winning, she also stopped asking Chloe for help.

Chloe also learned about her ancestors. She never knew her father's parents. They had died before she was born. She did know her mother's parents, however, and it was from them that she heard stories about what it was like growing up in the South. Chloe's great-grandparents were slaves before the Civil War (1861–1865). Her grandfather was not yet five years old when he heard his parents talking about something called the emancipation. He had no idea what it was, but it seemed to him that his parents became anxious whenever they talked about it, so he thought it must be something terrible. When he heard it was actually coming, he hid under the bed, unaware that it was Lincoln's Emancipation Proclamation that would lead to the end of slavery in the United States.

Chloe's grandparents also told her about their move north from Greenville, Alabama. In Alabama, they had been sharecroppers, which meant that they farmed for a landowner and were paid very little for their work. The family was in a constant state of poverty. Chloe's grandfather had to find other jobs to supplement their income.

One of those jobs took him to Birmingham, Alabama, where he used his violin to earn money as a musician. Morrison says:

> He sent money back, but my grandmother began to get nervous all alone in Greenville, because her daughters were reaching puberty and that was a dangerous business in the South, in the country, because white boys began to circle. So my grandmother decided to leave.[11]

She sent a verbal message to her husband, saying: "We're heading north on the midnight train. If you ever want to see us again, you'll be on that train."[12] It was a courageous thing to do. She had no way of knowing if her husband had gotten the message, and she had only $18 in her pocket. Still, she gathered her children and boarded the train.

As the train left the station, there was no sign of her husband, and the children began to cry. It was not until they were on their way that they saw him. He had been on the train all along but remained hidden because he was afraid someone would recognize him and not let him leave, because he owed money.

Chloe's family was very close and dependent on one another. Everyone in the family had work to do, and the others expected each person to take his or her responsibilities seriously. If Chloe was told to watch the food on the stove, she knew she had to do it. If she did not, the food would burn, and there was no more food to replace it.

When Chloe's grandfather got older, he would sometimes get confused and wander away from home. Chloe was sent to find him and bring him back. When her grandmother was dying, Chloe sat by her bedside reading to her from the Bible. Morrison says children then were taught how to care for adults. It was part of knowing who they were and where they came from.

Starting when she was twelve years old, Chloe worked at jobs to help with the family's finances. When she was thirteen, she had an after-school job cleaning house for a white family. It was not always easy. She remembered coming home one day complaining to her father that the woman was mean and the work was hard. Her father said, "Girl, you don't live there. You live *here*. So you go do your work, get your money and come on home."[13] His words made a lasting impression on Chloe, who learned that how she felt about herself was not determined by other people.

A graduation photo of Chloe Wofford (Toni Morrison) as it appeared in the 1949 Lorain High School yearbook

It was not only Morrison's family who guided her childhood. At that time, the community also took part in raising its children. People on the street felt comfortable correcting Chloe if they thought it was needed. "If I was misbehaving somewhere, put on lipstick too soon, they felt not only free but obliged to tell me not to do it . . ." she said.[14] However, as a teenager, she did not always appreciate all that guidance. "That was also something that made me feel, oh, boy, wait till I get out of this place, because I am tired of all these people who can meddle with me."[15]

Chloe attended Lorain High School where she was inducted into the National Honor Society. By then she was reading all the great Russian and French novels as well as novels by English writer Jane Austen and American novelists Ernest Hemingway, Willa Cather, and William Faulkner. They were not the type of books with which an African-American teenager could identify, but she loved them because they were so well written.

Chloe graduated from high school in 1949 and was accepted at Howard University in Washington, D.C. She became the first woman in her family to go to college. Her mother took a job as a ladies' room attendant to help pay for Chloe's education.

3

An Unanswered Prayer

t Howard University, Chloe Anthony Wofford began using the nickname "Toni." She said people seemed to have trouble pronouncing Chloe. Toni was a more familiar name.

She chose English as her major, but although Howard University was a predominantly black school, she had few opportunities to study the works of African-American writers. Most of the curriculum centered around classics written by white English and American authors, such as William Shakespeare, Herman Melville, and Nathaniel Hawthorne.

She soon became bored with the social life on

campus, which she said revolved around clothes and parties. Popularity appeared to depend on how much money a person had. To illustrate that point, Morrison once told an interviewer a story about a girl she knew at Howard University.

Morrison said:

> I liked her a lot, but she had no dates, and wasn't popular. She didn't care, she had a boy back home whom she liked and eventually married. But during her senior year, her parents came to visit her. They turned out to be very wealthy, and good God, she was overwhelmed. Suddenly all the dudes on campus, in their white jackets with their stethoscopes dangling out of their pockets, started coming around. They had a rush on that poor girl for the last six months.[1]

An activity Morrison did enjoy was a theater group called the Howard University Players. She took part in several on-campus productions, and during the summers the group traveled all over the South performing in plays.

Traveling with the Howard University Players gave Morrison her first opportunities to see the South, but she was not exposed to the racial violence that her father had seen there. "Our audiences were almost completely black. You really didn't come into contact with white people," she later explained.[2]

Morrison graduated from Howard University in 1953 with a bachelor of arts degree in English literature and a minor in the classics. She went on to Cornell

Toni Morrison displayed her acting ability in a production of *King Richard III* presented by the Howard University Players.

A photograph of Chloe Wofford (Toni Morrison) which appeared in the 1953 edition of the Howard Bison Yearbook

University in Ithaca, New York, where she earned a master of arts degree in English in 1955.

Morrison then accepted a position to teach English at Texas Southern University in Houston, Texas. "I was partly drawn to teaching because I didn't know what to do with a master's in English," she said. "Once I got into it, I really enjoyed it."[3]

After spending a year and a half in Texas, she returned to Howard University in 1957 to teach English. The following year she married Harold Morrison, an architect from Jamaica. At that time, she became known as Toni Morrison. Their son, Harold Ford, was born in 1961. His parents called him by his middle name, Ford.

At Howard University, as with other campuses all across the United States, the civil rights movement was gaining momentum. Morrison says she did not get too involved with politics at that time. One reason was because she was busy taking care of her young son. Another reason was that she did not agree with some of the changes civil rights leaders supported, particularly integration.

In 1954, the Supreme Court handed down its decision in *Brown* v. *Board of Education of Topeka*, ruling that racial segregation in the public schools was unconstitutional.

In 1955, the Supreme Court issued its implementation decree that the public schools be desegregated

This aerial view shows the Howard University campus, where
Toni Morrison attended college and later returned as a teacher
in 1957.

"with all deliberate speed." However, by the early
1960s, many school districts were still segregated.

Supporters of integration said it would give African-
American children a chance for a better education.
Morrison did not agree. She said:

> I was not in favor of integration. But I couldn't
> officially say that, because I knew the terror and the
> abuses of segregation. But integration also meant that

we would not have a fine black college or fine black education. I didn't know why the assumption was that black children were going to learn better if they were in the company of white children.[4]

Morrison believed that a better plan would be to put money into the schools in African-American neighborhoods so they would be able to buy educational materials and staff their schools with qualified teachers.

Morrison had not thought about becoming a writer, but she did like to read. It was that interest that drew her to a writers' group on campus in 1962. About ten writers, mostly poets, met once a month to read and critique each others' work. Their one rule was that everyone had to bring something they had written to read at each meeting.

At first Morrison read things she had written in high school. Then one month she did not have anything to bring. She hurriedly wrote a story about an African-American girl who longed to have blue eyes.

The idea for the story came from a conversation Morrison remembered having with another girl when they were children. The girl had said she did not believe in God because she had prayed for blue eyes for two years and never got them. Morrison tried to imagine what the girl would look like with blue eyes. She decided it was a good thing the girl's prayers had not been answered:

I always thought she was beautiful. I began to write
about a girl who wanted blue eyes and the horror of
having that wish fulfilled; and also about the whole
business of what is physical beauty and the pain of that
yearning and wanting to be somebody else. . . .[5]

Morrison read the story to her writers' group and
got positive responses from some of the members.
After that meeting, she put the story aside. She had no
plans to do anything more with it.

Morrison was expecting her second child when she
resigned from Howard University in 1964 and went to
Europe for the summer with her husband and their
son, Ford. Morrison and her husband separated while
they were in Europe. They later got a divorce.

Morrison has not talked much about her marriage.
However, in an interview with Collette Dowling of *The
New York Times*, she did give some insight into the dif-
ficulties of their relationship. "Women in Jamaica are
very subservient in their marriages," she said. "They
never challenge their husbands. I was a constant nui-
sance to mine. He didn't need me making judgments
about him, which I did. A lot."[6]

Harold Morrison returned to Jamaica, and Toni
Morrison remained with a small son, a baby on the
way, and no job. She went home to her family in
Lorain, Ohio, to have her baby. Her second child was
also a son—Slade Kevin Morrison.

Morrison could have stayed in Ohio and let her

family help raise her children, but she wanted to make it on her own. She remembers:

> It was a little bleak at that time. My back was up against the wall, and I didn't want the easy route, which was to live at home with my family or to be in another dependent situation. I wanted to find out who I was and whether I was tough enough.[7]

Her opportunity came when she saw an ad in *The New York Review of Books* for an editing position with a textbook publisher in Syracuse, New York. "The civil-rights movement was putting pressure on schools to revise the way blacks were being presented in the curriculum," she said. "I thought I might be able to make some changes."[8]

Morrison and her sons moved to Syracuse in 1965, and it was there that she began to get serious about writing. "I had two small children in a strange place and I was very lonely," she said. "Writing was something for me to do in the evenings, after the children were asleep."[9] She pulled out her story about the African-American girl who longed for blue eyes and began working on it again, expanding it into a novel.

4

THE BLUEST EYE

n 1967, Morrison was promoted to senior editor for the parent company of the publishing house where she worked. Her new position meant that instead of editing textbooks she would be working on mass-market books—those intended for the general book-buying public. Her promotion also meant a move from Syracuse, New York, to New York City where the publisher's headquarters were located.

In the meantime, Morrison continued to work on her own novel titled *The Bluest Eye*. When she had written about three-fourths of her book, she sent it to an editor at a different publishing house. The editor liked what Morrison had written so far and encouraged her to finish it. That editor was eventually responsible for getting the book published in 1970.

Although Morrison was an editor for a large publishing house, her book was published by another company. In an interview, Morrison explained how it happened that she became an editor for one publisher and a writer for another. "In the beginning I felt my employers would not look kindly on my attempts to publish a novel, so I was very secretive about my writing," she said. "They hired me to acquire novels, not write them."[1]

The Bluest Eye shows how racial prejudice can affect a child. It tells the story of three African-American girls—nine-year-old Claudia McTeer, her ten-year-old sister Frieda, and their eleven-year-old friend Pecola Breedlove. Morrison says she wanted to write a book about the culture in which she grew up and the African-American girls with which she identified. According to Morrison, African-American girls had been largely ignored in the world of literature. They appeared in novels only as peripheral characters— props. In Morrison's book, they took center stage.

The story takes place in 1941 in a small, midwestern town, which Morrison admits is patterned after Lorain, Ohio, her own hometown. "I think most first novels are pretty autobiographical in some way because you are frightened to pull from too many places," Morrison said.[2]

She used actual streets and landmarks from her hometown in the book, but she changed obvious things like people's names. However, Morrison says that people visiting Lorain today would not see the same things she wrote about in her book. Hers is a remembered version of her hometown.

Morrison also used bits and pieces of actual events from her childhood. She drew on observations she had made while she was a teenager working as a maid to write about Pecola's mother, Pauline. Morrison explained:

> In *The Bluest Eye*, Pauline lived in this dump and hated everything in it, And then she worked for the Fishers, who had this beautiful house, and she loved it. She got a lot of respect as their maid that she didn't get anywhere else. [3]

Much of *The Bluest Eye* is told from the point of view of Claudia McTeer, who began her story with words Morrison heard many times when she was growing up—"Quiet as it's kept . . ."[4] It means that a secret is about to be told. It was a phrase used by the African-American women Morrison knew when they were about to share a piece of gossip.

On the other hand, other parts of *The Bluest Eye* are nothing at all like Morrison's own experiences. Her own life was only a taking-off point for her writing. "Writing has to do with the imagination," she says.[5]

The novel opens with a paragraph from a basic reading series that at one time was widely used in the schools. Millions of children learned to read using those books about a brother and sister named Dick and Jane who lived with their dog and cat in a pretty green and white house where everyone was always happy. "The primer with white children was the way life was presented to the black people," Morrison said.[6]

She wanted to distort that image. She began with a passage from one of the readers. That paragraph is then repeated twice. The first time, the passage is double-spaced with the capitalization and punctuation all in place as it should be. Then it is repeated with no punctuation or capital letters, and the lines are closer together. The second time the passage is repeated, the lines are even closer together, and there is no space between the words. The paragraph has become almost unreadable. Throughout the book, there are other passages from the Dick and Jane readers that foretell the events in the section of the book that follows.

In the first few pages of her novel, Morrison told what happened—Pecola was pregnant with her father's baby, and the baby was born early and died. "It doesn't matter what happens," Morrison says.[7] What is important in her story is *why* it happened. Morrison's writing style had roots in the African-American oral history tradition where there was a back-and-forth conversation between the storyteller and the audience. She wanted that kind of response from her readers. "My writing expects, demands participatory reading, and that I think is what literature is supposed to do," she said. "It's not just about telling the story; it's about involving the reader."[8]

In the book, Claudia is an adult looking back on her childhood trying to understand how she and her sister were able to thrive during their childhoods in the neighborhood while their friend Pecola could not. Like Pecola, Claudia and Frieda McTeer came from a poor home, but unlike Pecola, they learned to love themselves because they were nurtured by their parents and neighbors.

Pecola, on the other hand, felt ugly and unloved—an opinion that was supported by her family and her community. At school, her teachers ignored her, and other students made fun of her. Pecola's mother preferred the blond-haired daughter of her white employer over her own daughter, and, in a final attack on her self-esteem, Pecola was raped by her drunken father.

Pecola decided that her ugliness was because she was black. She was fascinated with a drinking cup that was decorated with the face of Shirley Temple—a popular motion-picture personality at the time. Shirley

Temple had blue eyes, light brown curly hair, and dimples. Pecola longed to be like that child star because everyone adored her. Pecola prayed for blue eyes and eventually escaped into insanity believing that they had been given to her.

When *The Bluest Eye* was published, Morrison was upset to see the name Toni Morrison on the cover. "My name is Chloe Wofford," she later explained. "Toni's a nickname."[9] However, she did understand why it happened.

Morrison had submitted her manuscript under the name of Toni Morrison because her editor knew her by that name. In the general excitement of having her first book published, she never thought to mention that she wanted her given name, Chloe Wofford, to appear on the cover of the book.

The Bluest Eye was reviewed in several well-known publications, including *The New York Times Book Review*, *Newsweek*, the *New Yorker*, and the *Chicago Tribune*. Most of the reviewers agreed that the book was an impressive first novel.

Critics praised Morrison's use of language, calling her style "poetic." Morrison, on the other hand, does not like to use the term "poetic" in describing her writing because she says it makes it sound as if the language is ornate or showy.[10]

What she tries to do is write in the language used by the people she knows. She said:

🔲🔲🔲

Toni Morrison's first novel, *The Bluest Eye,* was published in 1970. At that time she was senior editor for a large publishing house in New York City.

When the language fits and it's graceful and powerful and like what I've always remembered black people's language to be, I'm ecstatic. It's always seemed to me that black people's grace has been with what they do with language. [11]

Reviewers also recognized early on that one of Morrison's strengths as a writer was the ability to write about villainous characters such as Pecola's father, Cholly Breedlove, in a way that made the reader feel sympathy for that character. In his critique for *The New York Times Book Review*, Haskel Frankel noted: "There are many novelists willing to report the ugliness of the world as ugly. The writer who can reveal the beauty and the hope beneath the surface is a writer to seek out and to encourage."[12]

It spite of positive reviews, the book had only modest sales. However, Morrison's life did change with the publication of her first novel. Because of her book, she became recognized as a critic and scholar of the African-American culture. Publications sought her opinions on African-American life and literature. Between 1971 and 1972, Morrison wrote twenty-eight book reviews for various publications. She also wrote an essay on how African-American women viewed the women's liberation movement. In that article, which appeared in *The New York Times* Magazine on August 22, 1971, Morrison said that the women's liberation movement primarily benefited white, middle-class women.

In 1971, Morrison accepted a position as a visiting professor of English at the State University of New York at Purchase. Being a visiting professor meant that Morrison made only a short-term commitment to the university. She agreed to teach there for that particular school year. She also continued editing.

Morrison says that after she finished writing *The Bluest Eye*, she went through a period of several months when she felt sad.[13] At first, she could not figure out why she felt that way, but eventually she realized she was missing her characters.

Morrison did not see herself as a novelist then. She had written her book and had no plans for another one. In fact, she did not even have an idea for another book until a character began to develop in her mind—a scandalous woman who did what she wanted instead of what people expected her to do. Then Morrison thought about another woman who was the exact opposite and wondered what it would be like if these two women were friends.

5

FRIENDSHIP AND EVIL

It took Morrison two and one-half years to write her second novel, _Sula,_ which was published in 1973. Morrison wrote much of it in her head while she commuted by subway from her home in Queens to her editing job in Manhattan. It was the only way to squeeze in time for her novel in a schedule that already included teaching, reviewing, editing, and being a single parent.

Morrison admitted that it was not always easy to juggle so many roles. In a 1994 interview she said, "I remember one day when I was confused about what I had to do next—write a review, pick up groceries, what?"[1] That day she took out a yellow pad and sat down and made a list of everything she had to get done. Then she made another list of the things she *wanted* to accomplish. Morrison says she discovered there were only two things she could not live without doing: raising her sons and writing books.

Morrison made time for writing by sacrificing her social life. "I don't do much. I don't go out. I don't entertain. And I get off the telephone," she explained.[2]

She also tried to do two things at once whenever possible. She could plan her manuscripts or solve a problem she was having with a book while she was driving the car, mowing the lawn, or washing dishes—jobs that did not take all of her attention. "Writing is a process that goes on all the time," Morrison said.[3]

For Morrison, the hardest part of writing came when she actually sat down and tried to work at home. She had two young sons who wanted and needed her attention. "It was very difficult writing and rearing children," Morrison remembers, "because they deserve all your time, and you don't have it."[4]

She noticed that if she wrote in a room away from her sons, they frequently interrupted her. On the other hand, if she worked in a room where they were busy with their own work or play, they did not interrupt her as much. So she wrote in a place where they could all be together and learned to tune out the noise around her.

In her second novel, Morrison explored the themes of friendship and evil. "When I wrote *Sula*, I knew I was going to write a book about good and evil and about friendship," she said. "I had to figure out what kind of people would manifest this theme, would have this kind of relationship."[5] She came up with two very different characters—Nel Wright and Sula Peace. Nel was conservative, and Sula was adventurous.

The book spanned the years 1919 to 1965, which included the beginning of their friendship when they were girls and continued on into their adult lives. As girls, they enjoyed their differences, but as they grew older, their lives took them in opposite directions. Nel accepted the path that women were expected to follow at that time. She married young and had a family.

Sula, on the other hand, was a rebel. She went off to college and then lived a mysterious life away from the community. When she returned ten years later, she still refused to conform to the rules of the community. She slept with other women's husbands and, finally, had an affair with Nel's husband, even though she did not love him. "I wanted to show the one thing that could break up such a friendship, and that was sexual betrayal," Morrison said.[6]

When Morrison wrote *Sula*, she was venturing into new territory. Until then, friendships between women had not been the main focus of a novel, although as Morrison noted, women had traditionally enjoyed such relationships. "People talk about the friendship of women, and them having respect for each other, like it's something new," she said. "But Black women have always had that, they always have been emotional life supports for each other."[7]

Unfortunately, because of her busy schedule, Morrison has not always had time to nurture her own friendships. "Sometimes I'll even forget to go if I've been invited to someone's house for dinner," she once told a reporter. "At this point in my life, anyone who's going to be a friend of mine is simply going to have to be able to understand that."[8]

The other theme Morrison wrote about in *Sula* was evil. However, she did not write about evil in traditional terms. "It was interesting to me that black people at one time seemed not to respond to evil in the ways other people did . . .'" Morrison said.[9] The African-American people she wrote about thought evil had a natural place in the universe. They protected themselves from it, but they never tried to get rid of it. Although African Americans in the community saw Sula as evil, they allowed her to live there peacefully.

Morrison dedicated *Sula* to her sons. They were only twelve and eight years old when the book was published, but she already realized how much she would miss them when they were grown. In her dedication, she wrote: "It is sheer good fortune to miss somebody long before they leave you. This book is for

Morrison with her sons Ford (left) and Slade. She dedicated her second novel, *Sula*, to them.

Ford and Slade, whom I miss although they have not left me."[10]

Sula was well received among critics, who called it "thought-provoking."[11] Reviewers also praised Morrison's dialogue and her ability to create interesting characters. In a review for *The New York Times*, Sara Blackburn wrote: ". . . her dialogue is so compressed and life-like that it sizzles."[12] In writing about Morrison's characters, Blackburn continued: ". . . it's hard to believe we haven't known them forever."[13]

However, not everyone shared Blackburn's opinion.

Other reviewers were critical of Morrison's characters. They said she had a tendency to write about ". . . pathetic, unusual, exotic community types."[14]

Morrison later addressed their comments in an interview. She said that she was drawn to what she called "extraordinary" people. She explained:

> In my family, there were some really interesting people who were willing to be whatever they were. People permitted it, perhaps because in the outer world the eccentrics had to be a little servant person or low-level factory worker. They had an enormous span of emotions and activities, and they are the people I remember when I go to write.[15]

There was also negative criticism about *Sula* from reviewers who were concerned about violence in the book. They cited particular scenes, including one where Sula as a child watched her mother burn to death without making any effort to help her. There was also Sula's grandmother, Eva Peace, who killed her own son because he had become a drug addict and she had decided that his life was not worth living.

Critics were not so much concerned that these episodes were in the book, but that Morrison wrote about such events without passing some kind of judgment on her characters. In a review for *The Nation*, Jerry H. Bryant stated that Morrison and other writers like her were ". . . slowly, subtly making our old buildings unsafe."[16] He went on to write: "There is something ominous in the chilling detachment with which they view their characters."[17]

Morrison is often dissatisfied with critics. She says some have not done a good job of studying her work because they do not consider the fact that she is writing about a culture that may be different from their own. "Critics of my work have often left something to be desired, in my mind," she said, "because they don't always evolve out of the culture, the world, the given quality out of which I write."[18] An example she gave was Sula's return to Medallion. To some critics, her return meant that she had failed because she was not able to survive in that outside world. However, Morrison says that in the African-American culture, Sula's return to where she came from could be seen as a triumph because she would be protected there.

An excerpt from *Sula* was featured in *Redbook* magazine, and the novel was nominated for the National Book Award. However, as with her first book, sales figures were not impressive.

After that book, Morrison put her writing on hold so she could focus on a book she was editing. It was a project that was important to her personally and professionally.

6

A CAREER TAKES FLIGHT

ne of Morrison's priorities as an editor was to help more African-American authors get published. She worked with many African-American writers, including Toni Cade Bambara, Gayl Jones, Andrew Young, and Henry Dumas. She also edited an autobiography by Angela Davis, a civil rights activist, and another one by boxing champion Muhammad Ali. However, the project that consumed so much of Morrison's attention after she finished writing *Sula* was a scrapbook covering three hundred years of African-American history.

Although Morrison's name does not appear

anywhere on that book, she was the one who came up with the idea for the project, and she spent eighteen months overseeing its development. Morrison said that there were other books that focused on African-American leaders. What she wanted to do was put together a book that told the history of African Americans "from the point of view of everyday people."[1]

To accomplish that goal, she relied on collectors of African-American memorabilia rather than writers. Middleton A. (Spike) Harris, a retired New York state parole officer, became her primary "author." Three other collectors—Morris Levitt, Roger Furman, and Ernest Smith—worked closely with him and were listed on the title page as contributors.

With Morrison's guidance, they put together a collection of old newspaper clippings, song lyrics, photographs, advertisements, patent office records, and excerpts from slave narratives. There was a section on dreams and how to interpret them and another section featuring voodoo recipes, including instructions on how to ward off evil spirits. Morrison also gathered materials from her own family and friends. She even had her cousin write a story about their family's migration north.

That collection, titled *The Black Book*, was published in 1974. "I am not sure what the project meant to the authors, but for me it was like growing up black one more time," Morrison said.[2]

In the meantime, Morrison had bought a house in Spring Valley, New York, and commuted daily to her editing job in Manhattan—a forty-five minute drive. Ford and Slade attended the United Nations International School in Manhattan. Each day Morrison dropped them off for school at 8:00 A.M. before she went to work. She was back to pick them up when school got out at 3:30 P.M., and then they all headed home for the day.

A reporter asked Morrison how she got her employer to agree to those hours. "You don't ask, you just do," she answered.[3]

It was the same philosophy she used in 1976 when Yale University offered her a position as a visiting professor for the 1976–77 school year. Her classes on the technique of fiction and the writings of African-American women were scheduled on Fridays so she could continue her work as an editor the rest of the week. Morrison said:

> I didn't ask anyone's permission to be out of the office on Fridays. I simply took the job. One day my boss announced that there'd be a production meeting or something on the following Friday. "I won't be able to be there," I told him. "I teach at Yale on Fridays."[4]

In 1977, her third novel, *Song of Solomon*, was published. That book about a man's search for his heritage brought Morrison national recognition as a writer.

Song of Solomon tells the story of Macon Dead, Jr., who was called "Milkman" because his mother, out of loneliness, nursed him long past the infant stage. Milkman's father was the richest man in town, having made his fortune as a ruthless landlord.

When Milkman was twelve years old, his Aunt Pilate, his father's sister, came to town. Pilate carried a bag of human bones and wore a brass box as an earring. She practiced voodoo and made her living by supplying bootleg whiskey to the town residents. While Macon Dead, Sr., accumulated wealth, Pilate lived with her daughter and granddaughter in a shack without modern conveniences. Macon Dead, Sr., was silent about his family's history, but Pilate cherished it. Milkman's father warned his son to stay away from Pilate, but Milkman ignored his father's wishes. It was through Pilate that Milkman began to learn about his past.

Morrison's first two books took place in small Ohio communities, but with *Song of Solomon*, she covered a larger area. Milkman set out on a journey to search for a bag of gold connected to his family's past. His travels took him from his home in Michigan to Pennsylvania and on to Virginia. However, instead of finding gold, he discovered his family's history, including the story of his great-grandfather Solomon who, they said, flew away from slavery. Morrison said:

That was always part of the folklore of my life; flying was one of our gifts. I don't care how silly it may seem. It is everywhere—people used to talk about it, it's in the spirituals and gospels. Perhaps it was wishful thinking—escape, death, and all that. But suppose it wasn't. What might it mean?[5]

It was an idea that Morrison wanted to explore in *Song of Solomon*. In the opening scene of the book, an insurance salesman attempted to fly by jumping from the hospital roof. On the same day, the first African-American baby was born in that hospital. That baby was Milkman who had a life-long fascination with learning to fly the way he had heard African-Americans were able to do.

The title of the book came from a song Milkman heard a group of children singing in Virginia. It was actually a reciting of the geneology of Milkman's great-grandfather, Solomon. Morrison notes that there was such a song in her family, too.

Morrison says writing is always difficult, but *Song of Solomon* was even more so. That was partly because of some of the circumstances in her life at that time. "My eldest son was entering manhood and if they do that properly, they do it explosively," Morrison told a reporter. She paused, then quipped, "He was doing it properly."[6]

Morrison admits that being a single parent is not easy. Although her sons saw their father occasionally, Toni Morrison did most of the parenting alone. "Of

Toni Morrison talks about her third novel, *Song of Solomon,* which was published in 1977.

course the ideal situation is to have a mother and father in the home," she says. "But if that doesn't happen, there's no reason to get bitter about it."[7]

She was able to feel good about the way she had learned to take charge of her life. "I used to hate to have to fix things myself," she explained. "But after I fixed it, I said, hey, *I* fixed that. What I'm trying to say is that I like myself better for having to take hold of my life, alone."[8]

Another circumstance that made writing hard for Morrison at that time was that her father had just died. "I was very depressed afterward—I knew that I no longer had a life that way: the way I lived in his mind," Morrison said.[9]

She struggled with her writing after her father died, but then she found that her writing was what eventually helped her through her grief. She recalled the day that she was finally able to work on her book again:

> I remember being filled with melancholy. I was sitting at my desk, my children were in the room. Suddenly I got this incredible feeling of exhilaration and serenity at the same time. I think because I was so depressed, my defenses were down, I wasn't fighting anything. And it was like a gate that opened in me. I began to envision the things in the book. I started writing and writing—I think I wrote 30 pages that night.[10]

Song of Solomon is told from a male point of view, which also made the writing more difficult for Morrison. For her, writing is a lot like being an actress. She tries to get inside her characters, to understand how they feel. Then she lets them act the way she thinks they would act rather than the way she wants them to act.

For *Song of Solomon*, Morrison drew from the things she knew about the men in her family. "I learned a lot from my sons," she said, "seeing how excited they got by going near danger, for instance— they'd come away *charged*, lifted, as if somebody'd turned the volume up."[11]

Morrison says she was also helped by her father, even though he had died. "I had long conversations with him in my head anyway . . ." she said.[12] The dedication of her book is simply one word: "Daddy."[13]

When *Song of Solomon* was published in 1977, Morrison resigned from her full-time editing position to concentrate on writing. It was a bold move for her to give up the security of her full-time job. A safer choice would have been to wait and see how well the book sold before making any changes, but Morrison wanted to make a commitment to writing. "I didn't want to be safe. I've never wanted only to be safe," she later said.[14] However, she did agree to do some part-time editing, working on four or five books a year. She still felt a need to bring more African-American authors to print.

Morrison's commitment to writing turned out to be a wise choice. Reviews of the book were positive. In a review for *Newsweek*, Margo Jefferson wrote: "*Song of Solomon* . . . is filled with suspense, family secrets and an intriguing mixture of history and legend. Morrison's earlier novels have received high praise; this one is being trumpeted as her major achievement."[15]

The book was featured on the front page of *The New York Times Book Review* and first serial rights were sold to *Redbook* magazine. *Song of Solomon* was also made a main selection of the Book-of-the-Month Club. Morrison was the first African-American author to have that distinction since Richard Wright's novel *Native Son* was named a main selection in 1940. *Song of Solomon* won the National Book Critics Circle Award in fiction for 1977 and became a best-seller in the paperback edition.

For Morrison, adjusting to fame was a new experience. "Being a writer I'm used to being the observer, not the other way around," she said.[16]

In an interview in the *Washington Post*, Morrison described the day that her new-found fame finally became a reality to her. She was taking her oldest son to his piano lesson that day. She dropped him off, and then, since there was not time to do much else, she decided to drive around until it was time to pick him up again. She drove past a bookstore and saw a display of her book in the window. "There was this huge sign in the window which said 'A Triumph' by Toni Morrison," she explained.[17] She realized then that it was actually her they were talking about.

Morrison said her success made it harder for her

to return to Lorain, Ohio, for visits with her family because the people she knew as she was growing up saw her in a different way. "It's awful when you go home and those women who all your life told you what to do, what to eat, what not to eat—just look at you," she said.[18] Morrison's mother, Ramah Wofford, and her sister, Lois, were still living in Lorain at that time. Her brothers, Raymond and George, lived nearby in Cleveland.

Morrison used earnings from *Song of Solomon* to buy a three-story renovated boathouse located in upstate New York on the Hudson River. It was about a thirty-minute drive from New York City where Morrison worked one day a week as a part-time editor. Ford and Slade transferred to a public school in the area, eliminating the need to commute to Manhattan for school.

The house featured a private dock on the river and a porch with a swinging wooden bench where Morrison sometimes wrote. Morrison remembered the first day she saw the house. She had walked out on the deck and was viewing the river, when she felt her father's presence. She thought he was telling her he approved of the house.[19]

Song of Solomon raised Morrison to a new level as a writer. However, she is realistic about the praise and awards she receives: ". . . it doesn't mean a thing when you're sitting in front of that typewriter, trying to think what comes after *The*," she said.[20]

7

POLITICS AND RACE

t was Morrison's fourth novel, *Tar Baby*, that landed her a spot on the cover of *Newsweek* magazine. She was only the second African-American woman to have that distinction. Another writer, Zora Neale Hurston, had appeared on the cover of *Newsweek* in 1943. The article about Morrison was published in the March 30, 1981, issue, shortly after *Tar Baby* was released.

Morrison worked on her fourth novel off and on for three and one-half years. "I would sometimes have three days in which I'd write day and night, especially during the summer, and then sometimes a week or

two when I wouldn't do anything but think about it,"
Morrison explained.[1]

She was not concerned that she might be
experiencing writer's block—a period of time when
authors find it impossible to write. She understood
that she was "blocked" because she was undecided
about something in her story. She knew that she just
had to wait and a solution would appear. "When I
read a book, I can always tell if the writer has written
through a block," Morrison explained. "If he or she
had just waited, it would have been better or different,
or a little more natural. You can see the seams."[2]

Morrison used the days when she was not writing
to tend to other parts of her life. When she was writing, everything else was put aside. She sometimes
got so wrapped up in her work that she would forget
appointments.

Tar Baby was based on a story from African-American
folklore that Morrison had heard as a child. Like most
folktales, there were several versions of that story about
Brer Rabbit and the Tar Baby. In an interview, Morrison
talked about the version she knew. In that story, a white
farmer made a tar baby and clothed it in a bonnet and
dress to trap a pesky rabbit that had been stealing
from the farmer's garden.

The rabbit saw the tar baby and said "Good morn-
ing," expecting to get a civilized response. The tar

baby did not answer, which made the rabbit so angry that he hit the tar baby and got stuck in the tar.

When the rabbit realized he was caught, he tried to outsmart the farmer. "Boil me in oil, skin me alive, but *please* don't throw me in that briar patch," the rabbit begged.[3]

The farmer fell for the trick and threw the rabbit in the briar patch. At the end of the story, the rabbit ran off, lickety-split, saying, "This is where I was born and bred at."[4]

Although the original story had a happy ending, it haunted Morrison. "I was always terrified by that story," she said, "and I never knew why."[5]

Much of the action in Morrison's fourth novel takes place on a Caribbean Island called Isle des Chevaliers. Morrison said she needed to have an isolated area for her story:

> In *Tar Baby* I wanted to be in a place where the characters had no access to any of the escape routes that people have in a large city. There were no police to call. There was no close neighbor to interfere. I wanted the characters all together in a pressure cooker, and that had to be outside of the United States.[6]

However, some scenes also branched out to other areas, such as New York City, Philadelphia, Paris, and a small town in northern Florida. It gave Morrison her largest writing canvas so far.

It was also the first time Morrison featured white

characters in a major role. They were Valerian Street, a retired candy manufacturer from Philadelphia, and his wife, Margaret. Sydney and Ondine Childs were their longtime African-American butler and cook.

The "tar baby" in Morrison's story was Jadine Childs, a well-educated Paris model. She was the niece and adopted daughter of Sydney and Ondine, but the Streets treated her like part of their own family. Jadine was indebted to the Streets because it was Valerian who paid for Jadine's education. That development in the story was part of Morrison's attempt to follow the tar baby theme. "In the original story, the tar baby is made by a white man—that has to be the case with Jadine," Morrison said.[7] Jadine had received a marriage proposal from a wealthy Frenchman and returned to Isle des Chavaliers to be with her family and think about her decision.

The rabbit was an African-American man named Son Green who was on the run from a manslaughter charge. He jumped ship and hid in the Street home for four days before he was caught. Although Son's presence upset other members of the household, Valerian Street decided to treat Son as a guest. He allowed Son to sleep in the guest room and eat meals with the family. Son was the catalyst who caused feelings of racism in both the black and white members of the household to surface.

As the story opened, the Streets were preparing to

celebrate Christmas at their vacation/retirement home on Isle des Chevaliers. They were hoping their son, Michael, would join them for the holidays even though, in the past, Michael had refused to come to the island. The reason he had stayed away is a mystery that unfolded as it became apparent that he was not going to come this time either.

While the secrets surrounding Michael's reluctance to spend time with his family were being exposed, Son and Jadine were falling in love. After the holidays, Son went to New York with Jadine. Jadine loved the city life, but Son was not comfortable there. He convinced Jadine to go with him to his hometown—Eloe, Florida. It was a small town, and Jadine was bored there. She decided that neither of them could live in the other's world and she ran, first to Isle des Chevaliers and then to Paris. At the end of the book, Son arrived on Isle des Chevaliers looking for Jadine. However, the ending is open-ended. The reader must decide if Jadine and Son can ever find happiness together.

Tar Baby received mixed reviews. In *Library Journal*, Janet Wiehe described *Tar Baby*: "A beautiful novel, equal in narrative power to the award-winning *Song of Solomon*."[8] In *Newsweek*, Jean Strouse wrote:

> . . . *Tar Baby* keeps you turning pages . . . a melodrama full of sex, violence, myth, wit, wry wisdom and the extraordinary sense of place that distinguishes all

Morrison's writing, it wraps its urgent messages in a highly potent love story.[9]

On the other hand, other critics said that the very qualities that made Morrison's other novels so extraordinary—lyrical prose and good dialogue—were overdone in *Tar Baby*. "A novelist's vice usually resembles his virtue, for what he does best he also tends to do to excess . . ." John Irving explained in a review for *The New York Times Book Review*.[10]

Others thought the book was too political. Morrison said she did not think *Tar Baby* was any more political than her other books. She thought the difference was that she had written about white characters in *Tar Baby*. "The politics of the other books were greater, but they were addressed only to Black people—it was obvious that it was a domestic affair," she said.[11]

In spite of mixed reviews, *Tar Baby* sold well. It made *The New York Times* best-seller list one month after it was published and stayed there for sixteen weeks. Morrison helped promote her book with a publishing tour through fourteen cities. She gave many television interviews, including an appearance on NBC's *Today* show.

In many of those interviews, the fact that Morrison was an African-American writer became an issue. It is a topic that Morrison has sometimes been unwilling to discuss because she says the question suggests that

African-American writers are inferior to other writers. "I mind talking about it when it appears as though I am a star within a diminished world," she explained. "On the other hand, I am very much a black writer; that is very much a part of what I do."[12]

Although Morrison does not always like to talk about being an African-American writer, she is able to laugh about it. While she was promoting *Tar Baby*, Morrison was interviewed on *The Dick Cavett Show* on PBS. Near the end of the taping of the show, Cavett asked if it would not have been nice to do the entire hour show without once mentioning the word *black*. Morrison smiled and answered, "I guess so, but you started it."[13]

Morrison's attitude toward interviews and reporters varies. Some of the words used to describe her are defensive, touchy, and prickly. Other reporters have found her to be warm, funny, and entertaining as she tells stories about her childhood and the people she knows. In an article for the *Chicago Tribune*, Dana Micucci wrote: "Her voice is soft and lulling, punctuated frequently by an exuberant laugh that hints of a warm and ready generosity."[14] When Betty Fussell interviewed Morrison for *Lear's* magazine, she wrote: "Toni Morrison does not so much give an interview as perform one, in a silken voice that can purr like a saxophone or erupt like brass."[15]

She does not disclose a lot of personal information in her interviews. "I probably spend about 60 percent of my time hiding," she once said. "I teach my children that there is a part of yourself that you keep from white people—always."[16]

One of the topics she will not discuss is any romantic involvements she has had since her divorce. However, she did talk about marriage and the fact that she has never remarried in an interview with Colette Dowling for *The New York Times Magazine*:

> What I like is the minutiae, the day-to-day stuff, the "Where are my socks?" I like *doing* things for a man. The trouble is, I don't have time for that kind of relationship anymore. The one time I did consider getting married, some years ago, the man expected me to go with him so he could take a job somewhere on the other side of the country. I thought he was crazy! All of a sudden it occurred to me, after not having been married for a while, that *that's* what that means: to be married, you have to go where they say.[17]

Morrison gave up her part-time editing position in 1983, and in 1984, she accepted a professorship at the State University of New York (SUNY) at Albany. There her writing took a detour when she was commissioned by the New York State Writers Institute at SUNY-Albany to write a play.

It was a risk. Few writers have been successful in switching from writing novels to plays, but Morrison thought she would be able to make the transition. She believed that one thing in her favor was that she wrote good dialogue, a necessary skill for playwriting.[18] Plus,

Morrison at a 1984 press conference at the State University of New York at Albany. The conference was held to announce that Morrison had accepted a professorship at the university.

she already had a story in mind, one that she had en-visioned as a play rather than a novel.

Morrison's play, *Dreaming Emmett*, was loosely based on the true story of Emmett Till. Till was a fourteen-year-old African-American boy from Chicago who had traveled south to Sumner County, Mississippi, to visit his uncle, the Reverend Moses Wright, during the summer of 1955.

On Wednesday, August 23, Till and his cousins had gone into a store to buy bubble gum. On the way out, Till said goodbye to the white woman behind the counter. Once they were out of the store, one of Till's cousins said, "Hey, don't you know you're not sup-posed to say goodbye to a white woman?"[19] Another cousin commented about how good-looking the woman was, and as they were walking away from the store, Till whistled, indicating to his cousin that he agreed.

A group of white men playing poker outside the store had watched the whole scene. They did not do anything then, but the following Sunday at 2:00 A.M. a group of white men, including the woman's husband, showed up at Reverend Wright's home. They took Till, under gunpoint, to a plantation twenty-five miles away. A witness saw Till with the men and later heard his cries for help as they began to beat him.

Three days later Till's body floated to the surface of a nearby river. He had been beaten and shot twice.

Toni Morrison visits with students on campus at the State
University of New York at Albany.

Although the body was badly mutilated, Till's mother said she knew it was him, and she identified a ring on his finger as one that her son wore.

The men were brought to trial but were found not guilty by an all-white male jury. Their defense was that the body discovered in the river was not Till's.

"The Emmett Till incident was a huge thing for me and for a lot of people," Morrison said.[20] Some people have said that it was the Emmett Till case that ignited the civil rights movement; Morrison does not agree. She said that came later, in December 1955, when Rosa Parks refused to give up her seat on a city bus in Montgomery, Alabama. Morrison said:

> The reason it never took off as a rallying cry for the civil rights movement was, I think, because of the sexual innuendo. Rosa Parks, on the other hand, was a nice woman, a maid, and she was tired and didn't want to sit in the back of the bus.[21]

Although Morrison based her play on a true story, she noted that it was not necessarily factual. "I like to make up stuff," she said. "I take scraps, the landscapes of something that happened, and make up the rest. I'm not interested in documentaries."[22] In Morrison's play, Till became a symbol for the high number of deaths through violence among urban African-American youths—a topic about which Morrison felt very strongly.

The play was directed by Gilbert Moses, a friend of

Morrison's. Among his previous credits were two segments of the *Roots* television miniseries. Morrison was very involved with the whole process of staging the play and attended many rehearsals.

Dreaming Emmett was performed on January 4, 1986, to celebrate the first time Dr. Martin Luther King, Jr.'s, birthday was to be recognized as a national holiday. The first Martin Luther King, Jr., Day was observed two weeks later.

Dreaming Emmett won the New York State Governor's Art Award. It also received good reviews, including one in *The New York Times* where Margaret Croyden wrote: "Toni Morrison's voice has been a powerful one in literature. Those working with her on *Dreaming Emmett* feel that she will now also be a powerful theatrical voice."[23] Whether or not Croyden's prediction would hold true, would not be answered right away. Morrison was focusing on another novel.

8

"SIXTY MILLION AND MORE"

orrison spent three years thinking about her fifth novel and another three years writing it. That book, *Beloved*, is about slavery. It was hard for Morrison to write about that time period. "I had this terrible reluctance about dwelling on that era," she said.[1]

It was also a difficult subject to research. Morrison found that there was not a lot of reliable information available on slavery. According to her, Americans have whitewashed the horrors of slavery, choosing not to remember it as it really was. Even slave museums, she notes, "are upbeat and cute," focusing on things like quilts slaves have made, rather than the grim realities of everyday life for American slaves.[2]

She said it was not just white people who tried to forget but black people as well. "In the move toward a life here, we didn't want to dwell on slavery," she explained. "You can't absorb it; it's too terrible. So you just try your best to put it behind you."[3]

However, Morrison saw a danger in not remembering. "You are condemned to repeat the mistakes if you do not fully understand them," she warned.[4]

Much of Morrison's research came from books written by slaves about their lives and the diaries of slave owners. She also did a lot of research in Brazil. Morrison says that although American slave museums had none of the chains or restraining devices used on slaves, museums in Brazil did. "I got a lot of help down there," she said.[5]

Morrison knew these devices had been used in America because slave owners wrote about them. In a diary of a slave owner named Byrd, the author frequently referred to something called the bit. "Put the bit on Jenny today," he wrote.[6] Morrison says the bit was like a metal tongue that was placed in the mouth of a slave. It was impossible to talk while wearing a bit, and it was painful. There were reports from slaves who were still nursing sore mouths two days after the bit was removed.

There were also masks that the slaves had to wear

Morrison at her upstate New York home where she worked on her fifth novel, *Beloved*.

when they cut sugar cane. It was supposed to keep them from eating any of what they harvested. In describing the masks, Morrison said, "They had holes in them, but it was so hot inside that when they took them off, the skin would come off."[7]

Morrison used this information as background for her book, but her main focus was on the people and the courage it took for a slave just to survive. She was not interested in writing about slaves in general. She wanted to give them names and make them real people. To do that, she needed to get inside her characters. "I had to feel what it might feel like for my own children to be enslaved," she said.[8]

What would it be like to have no control over your future? she wondered. What were the risks of trying to get control of your own life? When slaves escaped from a plantation, they never knew where they would be safe. There were people who would help them and people who would kill them. Fugitive slaves had no way of knowing which was which. Every contact with another person was a risk.

Morrison also tried to understand how it would feel to have no family. "Slavery depends on the absence of a family," Morrison said.[9] Families represent strength—a willingness to fight for and protect one another. If slave masters were to have complete control over their slaves, family life had to be destroyed. Husbands and wives were separated. Slave children were taken from their mothers and sold to other plantation owners. Mothers never saw their children again.

The idea for *Beloved* came from an article published in *The American Baptist* in 1856. Morrison read it when she was editing *The Black Book*, which was released in 1974.

The article told the story of Margaret Garner, a slave who escaped with her four children and settled in a small neighborhood outside of Cincinnati, Ohio. At that time, in 1856, the Fugitive Slave Bill was in effect. It said that if slaves ran away, they could be hunted down and taken back.

According to the article, slave hunters discovered where Garner was hiding, and they came to get her and her children. When Garner realized they were about to be caught, she tried to kill her children. She hit two of them with a shovel, injuring them. She succeeded in killing a third child by slitting her throat. Garner was stopped before she could do anything to the fourth child.

A reporter for the *American Baptist* interviewed Garner in her jail cell. Garner calmly explained to the reporter that she would rather kill her children quickly and end their suffering than to ". . . have them taken back to slavery, and be murdered by piece-meal."[10] Other reporters got the same response. "All the people who interviewed her kept saying she was very quiet, she was very serene," Morrison noted.[11]

Morrison did not do any further research on Garner because she wanted to be able to fictionalize Garner's story. She began to imagine . . . What if the child Garner had killed returned and remembered what had happened? What if she was angry about what her mother had done?

Beloved tells the story of Sethe, a slave who arranged for her children's escape and then managed to escape herself from the Sweet Home Plantation in Kentucky. She made her way to her mother-in-law's home outside of Cincinnati, Ohio. Sethe was pregnant at the time, and her daughter, Denver, was born during that journey.

The book begins in 1873, eighteen years after Sethe's escape. The Civil War had ended and the slaves had been freed. Sethe and Denver lived alone in the house at 124 Bluestone Road. At one time, Sethe also shared the home with her two sons and her mother-in-law Baby Suggs. However, as the story opened, Baby Suggs had recently died, and Sethe's two sons had left home to get away from the ghost who haunted their house. The ghost was Sethe's other daughter, who was murdered when she was only two years old. Who murdered her? How? And why? The answers to these questions were a mystery until Paul D, another former slave from the Sweet Home Plantation, arrived, and he and Sethe began to exchange stories from the past.

Paul D moved in with Sethe and Denver. He chased the ghost away, and it looked like the three of them were going to be able to live together as a family. Then a young woman walked out of the pond behind the house and took over their home. She called herself Beloved. Sethe, Paul D, and Denver believed the woman was Sethe's daughter who had been reincarnated in the body of a woman the age she would have been had she lived.

Beloved is not written in chronological order but instead is told through the characters' memories. Morrison wanted her writing to reflect the way people remember. The characters recall bits and pieces of information from here and there. In some cases, there are gaps in a character's memory—they may not know what happened later—and another person is able to fill in the missing pieces. There are also different versions of the past, depending on the character's point of view. Through these memories, the reader learns about life on the Sweet Home Plantation, how Paul D and Sethe each managed to escape, what became of the other slaves from Sweet Home, including Sethe's husband, and the circumstances surrounding the death of Sethe's daughter.

The reincarnated Beloved also had memories and wanted answers from her mother about the past. However, it became apparent in the book that she had not only her own memories, but those of her ancestors, including memories of Africans who died during the boat trip to America.

Morrison says it was especially hard for her to find research information about the journey by boat from Africa to America. There were no stories handed down orally from slaves. The trip was so terrible, they did not want to remember it.

Most of the information she got came from ship's captains who felt compelled to write their life stories before they died. Morrison also read accounts written by travelers who described the difficulty boats had navigating the Congo River in Africa because the river was jammed with bodies. They were the corpses of Africans who had been captured by slave traders but had died before they even got out of Africa. "They packed 800 into a ship if they'd promised to deliver 400," Morrison said. "They assumed that half would die. And half did."[12]

Morrison dedicated her book to the "Sixty Million and more"[13] black Africans who never even survived the trip to slavery. In an interview for *Time* magazine, Bonnie Angelo asked Morrison if that number was accurate. "Some historians told me 200 million died," Morrison answered. "The smallest number I got from anybody was 60 million."[14]

Morrison thought there needed to be some kind of a memorial to slaves. She noted that in the South most small towns had a monument to a Confederate hero.

"But there's not one memorial or haven or park dedicated to slaves, the survivors," she said.[15] Her book became that monument.

Beloved was released in September 1987, and it made *The New York Times* best-seller list that first week. Three weeks later, it was number three on the list, an unusual feat for a book of serious, rather than popular, fiction.

Reviews were positive. In a review for *Newsweek*, Walter Clemons predicted: "I think we have a masterpiece on our hands here . . ."[16] In *The New York Times Book Review*, Margaret Atwood wrote: "*Beloved* is Toni Morrison's fifth novel, and another triumph."[17]

Hope Hale Davis reviewed the book for *The New Leader* and praised Morrison's ability to pull the reader into the book. She noted that Morrison had written about an important part of Civil War history:

> We realize this only gradually, though, after she has already made us part of it—made us love, lose, endure, resist, take flight, murder, and struggle against memories that have become ours. Being one with people who were not regarded as people, we learn what living intensely means, and we will never be the same again.[18]

As a memorial or a reminder of the horrors of slavery, the book was equally successful. Critics compared *Beloved* to books written about the Holocaust—the mass execution of European Jews in

Nazi concentration camps before and during World War II (1939–1945).

Yet even among the critics who praised Morrison's book, there were some reviewers who had trouble accepting the reincarnation of Sethe's daughter. In *Vogue* magazine, Carol E. Rinzler critiqued:

> . . . Morrison takes unusual chances with this novel, blurring the boundaries of life and death, of reality and fantasy, which requires a considerable suspension of disbelief on the part of her reader. Perhaps she does not provide the help necessary to sustain it.[19]

Morrison said the idea of reincarnation was not foreign in the early days of the African-American culture. She thought it seemed to fit into the time period she was writing about.

Beloved did not win the National Book Award or the National Book Critics Circle Award, two important national prizes for writers. Other African-American authors and scholars were outraged by the snub. They got together and published a letter of protest in *The New York Times Book Review*.

"Despite the international stature of Toni Morrison, she has yet to receive the national recognition that her five major works of fiction entirely deserve. . . ." they wrote.[20] The letter signed by forty-eight African-American writers and scholars was published on January 24, 1988.

From Morrison's point of view, the best part about

Morrison, winner of the 1988 Pulitzer Prize in fiction, receives her award from Columbia University President Michael I. Sovern. The ceremony took place at the university on May 23, 1988.

that show of support from her peers was that so many African Americans had joined together to voice their opinion about something that mattered to them.

Less than three months later, on April 1, 1988, it was announced that Morrison had been selected to receive the Pulitzer Prize for fiction. Many supported the committee's choice; however, there were others who thought the decision had been partly politically motivated because of the letter published in *The New York Times*.

Morrison downplayed the importance of winning the Pulitzer Prize. She said that she was flattered but that it did not really change her life. "My rank in terms of writing is of no interest to me," she said.[21]

9

THAT "DIRTY, GET-ON-DOWN MUSIC"

 ardening is Toni Morrison's only one real hobby. Writing, lecturing, and teaching leave her little time for anything more. However, the lack of free time does not seem to bother her. "My work is my fun . . . my work is what I would do if I had everything I wanted," she says.[1] When *Beloved* was published, she was fifty-six years old and busier than ever.

According to reports, Morrison was receiving between five and six hundred requests a year for speaking engagements all across the country. From that number, she chose one or two requests a month to accept.[2]

There was also her teaching. In January 1989, Morrison left her position at the State University of New York at Albany and went to Princeton University where she had accepted the Robert F. Goheen chair. With that move, she became the first African-American writer to hold a named chair at an Ivy League university.

A chair at a university is the chief executive officer of a department. It is usually more prestigious to have a named chair which is established to honor someone important to the university. Robert F. Goheen had been a president at Princeton University.

Morrison bought a house in Princeton, New Jersey, and divided her time between it and her upstate New York home, which she used as a retreat. She also had an apartment in New York City.

Morrison had her biggest publishing year ever in 1992 with the release of three new books, including her sixth novel, *Jazz*, which was published that spring. *Jazz* is set in the Harlem section of New York City in the mid-1920s. Morrison says she was inspired to write about that time period because of the stories her parents had told her about when they were younger.

Jazz is a type of music known for its improvisation, which means that musicians create music as they play. Because of that spontaneity, each performance is

Toni Morrison smiles for reporters on the Princeton University campus. At Princeton, she is the Robert F. Goheen chair.

different, giving the music a special excitement. During the 1920s, a period nicknamed the Jazz Age by novelist F. Scott Fitzgerald, jazz was especially popular, and the Harlem neighborhood of New York City was an important jazz center.

Morrison says the idea for *Jazz* came from a book of photographs taken by James Van der Zee titled *The Harlem Book of the Dead*. One of the photographs was of an eighteen-year-old girl lying in a coffin. Morrison learned that the girl in that photograph had gone to a party and was dancing, when suddenly she slumped to the floor. The people around her noticed blood, but no one knew what had happened. They asked her, but all she would say was that she would tell them the next day. She died during the night.

No one knew she had been shot until after she had died. They discovered that her jealous boyfriend had shot her, using a gun with a silencer. The girl had refused treatment, telling everyone she would explain the next day, but what she was really doing was giving the boyfriend time to get away.

In the first paragraph of *Jazz*, an unnamed narrator told about a woman she knew. "Know her husband, too," the narrator said. "He fell for an eighteen-year-old girl with one of those deepdown, spooky loves that made him so sad and happy he shot her just to keep the feeling going."[3] Later, the man's wife, Violet, went to the funeral and tried to slash the

A photograph of Toni Morrison from 1992, taken the same year that her novel *Jazz* was published.

dead girl's face. The man was Joe Trace, a door-to-door cosmetics salesman, and his teenage lover was named Dorcas.

The narrator went on to explain why Joe was never brought to trial for killing Dorcas:

> There was never anyone to prosecute him because nobody actually saw him do it, and the dead girl's aunt didn't want to throw money to helpless lawyers or laughing cops when she knew the expense wouldn't improve anything.[4]

Knowing what has happened, the next question is "Why?" Morrison answered that through flashbacks that gave insights into the past of each of her characters. Each of them had lost someone. Joe Trace was abandoned by his parents when he was a child, and Violet's mother committed suicide because she was tired of living in poverty. Dorcas was orphaned when her parents were killed in riots in St. Louis. *Jazz* is also about survival, and Morrison showed the healing process that Joe and Violet went through as they began to put their lives back together.

The word "jazz" does not appear anywhere in the book, but the music is an important part of Morrison's Harlem setting. Morrison wrote about the men who sat in open windows or on rooftops blowing on their horns and the ". . . belt-buckle tunes vibrating from pianos and spinning on every Victrola."[5]

There were also the women who blamed the music

for the violence in their neighborhood—"The dirty, get-on-down music the women sang and the men played and both danced to, close and shameless or apart and wild."[6]

In a review for *New Statesman & Society*, Andrea Stuart noted how important music was in the telling of Morrison's story. "You do not read this book; you listen to it," she wrote.[7]

Jazz has no final chord. As a result, it keeps listeners on the edge of their chairs always anticipating more. "There is always something else that you want from the music. I want my books to be like that—because I want that feeling of something held in reserve and the sense that there is more—that you can't have it all right now," Morrison said.[8]

Although some critics said Morrison's lyrical, or musical, style of writing was overdone in this book, most reviewers were enthusiastic in their praise of *Jazz*. In *Maclean's*, Diane Turbide wrote: ". . . Morrison has again proven to be a formidable storyteller."[9] In a review for *Vogue*, Jane Smiley wrote: "It is a novel that should be read with pleasure and wonder."[10]

Jazz was one of two books Morrison had published that spring. The other was a book of literary criticism titled *Playing in the Dark: Whiteness and the Literary Imagination*. The three essays that make up the book had originally been presented as a series of lectures given by Morrison at Harvard University in 1990.

According to Morrison, literary historians and critics in the past had ignored the subject of race in their critiques of early American literature. In her essays, Morrison examined the racial attitudes of several early American writers, including Willa Cather, Edgar Allan Poe, Mark Twain, and Ernest Hemingway. "Black characters were used to represent endless love, like Jim in *Huckleberry Finn*, for example," Morrison said.[11]

Both *Playing in the Dark* and *Jazz* made *The New York Times* best-seller list that spring. It was an unusual occurrence for an author to have two books on the best-seller list at the same time in two different categories—fiction and nonfiction.

Morrison edited and contributed to another book of essays that was published that fall. The rather lengthy title of the book was *Race-ing Justice, En-Gendering Power: Essays on Anita Hill, Clarence Thomas, and the Construction of Social Reality.*

The confirmation hearings of United States Supreme Court Justice nominee Clarence Thomas took place in October 1991. Anita Hill, a University of Oklahoma law professor, challenged Thomas's appointment, accusing him of having sexually harassed her in the past. Thomas denied her charges, and there was no way to determine who was telling the truth. In the end, the United States Senate confirmed Thomas's appointment, but the hearings left questions unanswered. People wondered if all the attention on Anita Hill's charges had covered up other issues that should have been considered in deciding on Thomas's appointment. Others expressed concerns about the way complaints of sexual harassment were viewed.

Morrison decided that there needed to be a collection of essays about the hearings, written by various academics to shed some light on those questions. *Race-ing Justice, En-Gendering Power* was published in October 1992. It includes eighteen essays plus an introduction written by Morrison.

A year later, on October 7, Morrison was notified that she had won the Nobel Prize for literature. In the announcement, the Nobel committee cited three books that had played a significant role in its decision—*Song of Solomon*, *Beloved*, and *Jazz*.

Morrison said that she was happy her mother, Ramah Wofford, was still alive to share her joy, especially since four other relatives had died that year. Her mother, who was then eighty-seven years old and living in a nursing home in Ohio, has died since then. Morrison's brother, George, died a few weeks after the announcement of the Nobel prize was made and before Morrison flew to Stockholm, Sweden, in December for the presentation.

Morrison's sister, Lois, and her sister's two daughters were able to travel to Stockholm.

Morrison's sons, Ford and Slade, were also there. Her sons were thirty-one and twenty-seven years old at that time and had careers of their own. Ford worked as a musician—playing flute and guitar—and as a sound engineer. Slade, like his father, became an architect.

In an interview, Morrison described how she felt about accepting the Nobel Prize. She said she was pleased that her success might inspire young African Americans:

> I felt the way I used to feel at commencements where I'd get an honorary degree: that it was very important for young black people to see a black person do that, that there were probably young people in South-Central Los Angeles or Selma who weren't quite sure that they could do it. But seeing me up there might encourage them to write one of those books I'm desperate to read. And *that* made me happy. It gave me license to strut.[12]

Less than three weeks after Morrison returned home from Sweden, a Christmas day fire destroyed her home along the Hudson River. The fire started when a spark from the fireplace ignited a couch. According to newspaper accounts, one hundred firefighters from nearby communities fought the blaze. Several firefighters suffered injuries, but no one in Morrison's family was hurt.

Morrison's son, Slade, was alone in the home when the fire started. He immediately called his mother at her home in Princeton, New Jersey. She hurried to

Morrison received the Nobel Prize in literature from Swedish King Carl XVI Gustaf in the Concert Hall in Stockholm, Sweden, on December 10, 1993.

her New York home, arriving in time to see the last of the firefighting efforts.

Historians and scholars feared that valuable papers and manuscripts had been lost in the fire. They later learned that most of her papers were in a basement study and had not been damaged.

Several months later Morrison still felt the effects of that fire. In an interview with Claudia Dreifus for *The New York Times Magazine*, Morrison said:

> When I think about the fire, I think I may not ever, ever, ever get over it. And it isn't even about the *things*. It's about photographs, plants I nurtured for 20 years, about the view of the Hudson River, my children's report cards, my manuscripts.[13]

Morrison did not make any immediate decisions about rebuilding. "Princeton's fine for me right now," she said. "I have wonderful students and good friends here. Besides, I'm in the middle of a new novel and I don't want to think about where I'm living."[14]

10

WRITING FOR LIFE

 orrison has continued to receive honors and awards for her work. On January 22, 1995, she returned to her hometown of Lorain, Ohio, where she attended ribbon-cutting ceremonies for a Toni Morrison Reading Room located in the Lorain Public Library.

On February 15, 1995, the New York chapter of Women in Communications, Inc., announced the recipients of the 1995 Matrix Awards. The Matrix Awards were established in 1970 to honor women who have distinguished themselves in the field of

als

The Toni Morrison Reading Room in the Lorain Public Library. Dedication ceremonies for the room were held on January 22, 1995.

communications. Toni Morrison was selected to receive that year's award for the category of books.

On March 2, 1995, Toni Morrison was feted by her alma mater, Howard University, and awarded an honorary degree—Doctor of Humane Letters. More than one thousand people turned out for the occasion.

Recognition and monetary success have been the rewards of Morrison's hard work, but they have never been a goal. "There's a difference between writing for a living and writing for life," Morrison told her creative writing students. "If you write for a living, you

Morrison receives a 1995 Matrix Award in a ceremony held in the Grand Ballroom of New York's Waldorf-Astoria Hotel on April 4, 1995.

make enormous compromises, and you might not ever be able to uncompromise yourself. If you write for life, you'll work hard; you'll do it in a disciplined fashion; you'll do what's honest, not what pays."[1]

Morrison has not compromised. In an interview she once shared her definition of a novel. "A novel ought to confront important ideas, call them historical or political, it's the same thing," she said. "But it has another requirement, and that is its art. And that should be a beautiful thing."[2]

By her own definition, Morrison has been successful as a novelist. She presents unforgettable characters in language that has been described as lyrical and rich. She invites her readers into her books to participate in the telling of her stories, and in the process, she challenges them to think about ideas they may not want to consider.

One of her readers once said:

> I buy a Morrison novel the first day it's put on the shelves. I trust her totally; I know that even if I don't agree with everything she says, it will be the consummate reading experience: a work written extremely well and about something I need to deal with.[3]

Her writing will continue to have an impact on American lives. Talk show hostess Oprah Winfrey has acquired the film rights to *Beloved* for her television-movie and feature-film business known as Harpo Films. Winfrey plans to cast herself in the role of Sethe in a movie based on that book. Director Spike Lee has optioned film rights to her book *Sula,* and a French-based production company has acquired the rights to *Tar Baby.* Meanwhile, Morrison continues to work on another novel that she says will be set in the 1970s. Morrison has had a tremendous impact in the literary world as an editor, a teacher, and a writer, and she serves as an inspiration for others, both black and white, who will follow in her footsteps.

CHRONOLOGY

1931—Born in Lorain, Ohio, on February 18.

1949—Graduated from Lorain High School.

1953—Received bachelor's degree in English from Howard University in Washington, D.C.

1955—Received master's degree in English from Cornell University in Ithaca, New York.

1955–1957—Taught English at Texas Southern University in Houston, Texas.

1957—Returned to Howard University as a teacher.

1958—Married Harold Morrison.

1961—Son Harold Ford was born.

1962—Joined a writers' group at Howard University.

1964—Resigned from Howard University; divorced Harold Morrison; son Slade Kevin was born.

1965—Accepted an editing position with a textbook publisher in Syracuse, New York.

1967—Promoted to senior editor for the company's parent company; moved to New York City.

1970—*The Bluest Eye* was published.

1971–1972—Was a visiting professor of English at the State University of New York at Purchase.

1973—*Sula* was released.

1974—*The Black Book* was published.

1976–1977—Taught at Yale University.

1977—*Song of Solomon* was published.

1981—*Tar Baby* was released.

1984—Accepted a professorship at the State University of New York at Albany.

1986—Morrison's play *Dreaming Emmett* was performed in Albany on January 4.

1987—*Beloved* was published.

1988—Received the Pulitzer Prize for fiction.

1989—Left her position at the State University of New York at Albany; accepted the Robert F. Goheen chair at Princeton University.

1992—Published sixth novel, *Jazz*, and a book of essays titled *Playing in the Dark: Whiteness and the Literary Imagination*; edited and contributed to another book of essays titled *Race-ing Justice, En-Gendering Power: Essays on Anita Hill, Clarence Thomas, and the Construction of Social Reality*.

1993—Won the Nobel Prize for literature.

1995—Attended dedication of the Toni Morrison Reading Room located in the Lorain Public Library in Lorain, Ohio; received a Matrix Award in the category of books; was awarded the degree Doctor of Humane Letters by her alma mater Howard University.

Chapter Notes

Chapter 1

1. William Grimes, "Toni Morrison Is '93 Winner of Nobel Prize in Literature," *The New York Times*, October 8, 1993, p. C32.

2. Ibid.

3. Liz McMillen, "Princeton's Toni Morrison Wins Nobel Prize in Literature," *The Chronicle of Higher Education*, October 13, 1993, p. A11.

4. Toni Morrison, "Nobel Lecture 1993" (transcript), *World Literature Today*, Winter 1994, p. 5.

5. David Gates with Danzy Senna and Lynn James, "Keep Your Eyes on the Prize," *Newsweek*, October 18, 1993, p. 89.

6. Mel Watkins, "Talk with Toni Morrison," *The New York Times Book Review*, September 11, 1977, p. 48.

Chapter 2

1. Paula Giddings, "The Triumphant Song of Toni Morrison," *Encore American & Worldwide News*, December 12, 1977, p. 27.

2. David Streitfeld, "The Laureate's Life Song," *Washington Post*, October 8, 1993, p. D1.

3. Judith Wilson, "A Conversation with Toni Morrison," *Essence*, July 1981, p. 130.

4. "Toni Morrison: O-o-o-ooh She 'Done Fly' into the Literary Top Rank with *Song of Solomon*," *People Weekly*, January 2, 1978, p. 84.

5. Colette Dowling, "The Song of Toni Morrison," *The New York Times Magazine*, May 20, 1979, p. 42.

6. Toni Morrison, "Behind the Making of *The Black Book*," *Black World*, February 1974, p. 87.

7. Anne Commire, ed., *Something About the Author, Volume 57* (Detroit: Gale Research, 1989), p. 136.

8. Ibid.

9. Ibid.

10. Christina Davis, "Interview with Toni Morrison," *Presence Africaine*, 1988, p. 144.

11. Jean Strouse, "Toni Morrison's Black Magic," *Newsweek*, March 30, 1981, p. 53.

12. Ibid.

13. Ibid., p. 54.

14. Amanda Smith, "Toni Morrison," *Publishers Weekly*, August 21, 1987, p. 50.

15. Ibid.

Chapter 3

1. Karen De Witt, "Toni Morrison's Saga of a Black Family Is Being Hailed in All the Proper Places," *Washington Post*, September 30, 1977, p. C3.

2. Rosemarie K. Lester, "An Interview with Toni Morrison," Hessian Radio Network, Frankfurt, Germany in *Critical Essays on Toni Morrison*, ed. by Nellie Y. McKay (Boston: G. K. Hall, 1988), p. 50.

3. Dana Micucci, "An Inspired Life: Toni Morrison Writes and a Generation Listens," *Chicago Tribune*, May 31, 1992, sec. 6, p. 3.

4. Lester, p. 51.

5. Charles Ruas, *Conversations With American Writers* (New York: Knopf, 1984), p. 218.

6. Colette Dowling, "The Song of Toni Morrison," *The New York Times Magazine*, May 20, 1979, p. 48.

7. Micucci, sec. 6, p. 3.

8. Dowling, p. 48.

9. Ibid.

Chapter 4

1. Edwin McDowell, "Behind the Best Sellers: Toni Morrison," *The New York Times Book Review*, July 5, 1981, p. 18.

2. Bessie W. Jones and Audrey L. Vinson, *The World of Toni Morrison: Explorations in Literary Criticism* (Dubuque, Iowa: Kendall/Hunt, 1985), p. 129.

3. Claudia Dreifus, "Chloe Wofford Talks About Toni Morrison," *The New York Times Magazine*, September 11, 1994, p. 73.

4. Toni Morrison, *The Bluest Eye* (New York: Holt, Rinehart and Winston, 1970), p. 3.

5. Claudia Tate, ed., *Black Women Writers at Work* (New York: Continuum, 1983), p. 127.

6. Thomas LeClair, "'The Language Must Not Sweat,'" *New Republic*, March 21, 1981, p. 29.

7. Tate, p. 125.

8. Ibid.

9. Dreifus, p. 74.

10. LeClair, p. 26.

11. Mel Watkins, "Talk with Toni Morrison," *The New York Times Book Review*, September 11, 1977, p. 48.

12. Haskel Frankel, "The Bluest Eye," *The New York Times Book Review*, November 1, 1970, p. 47.

13. Danille Taylor-Guthrie, ed., *Conversations With Toni Morrison* (Jackson: University Press of Mississippi, 1994), p. 206.

Chapter 5

1. Claudia Dreifus, "Chloe Wofford Talks About Toni Morrison," *The New York Times Magazine*, September 11, 1994, p. 75.

2. Claudia Tate, ed., *Black Women Writers at Work* (New York: Continuum, 1983), p. 119.

3. Ibid., p. 120.

4. Dana Micucci, "An Inspired Life: Toni Morrison Writes and a Generation Listens," *Chicago Tribune*, May 31, 1992, sec. 6, p. 3.

5. Tate, p. 118.

6. Cathleen Medwick, "People Are Talking About . . . : Toni Morrison," *Vogue*, April 1981, p. 331.

7. Paula Giddings, "The Triumphant Song of Toni Morrison," *Encore American & Worldwide News*, December 12, 1977, p. 30.

8. Colette Dowling, "The Song of Toni Morrison," *The New York Times Magazine*, May 20, 1979, p. 54.

9. Tate, p. 129.

10. Toni Morrison, *Sula* (New York: Knopf, 1973), dedication page.

11. Jessie Carney Smith, ed., *Epic Lives: One Hundred Black Women Who Made a Difference* (Detroit: Visible Ink Press, 1993), p. 384.

12. Sara Blackburn, "Sula," *The New York Times Book Review*, December 30, 1973, p. 3.

13. Ibid.

14. Elaine Showalter, ed., *Modern American Women Writers* (New York: Scribner, 1991), p. 326.

15. Thomas LeClair, "'The Language Must Not Sweat'," *New Republic*, March 21, 1981, p. 28.

16. Jerry H. Bryant, "Something Ominous Here," *The Nation*, July 6, 1974, p. 24.

17. Ibid.

18. Nellie McKay, "An Interview with Toni Morrison," *Contemporary Literature*, Winter 1983, p. 425.

Chapter 6

1. Toni Morrison, "Rediscovering Black History," *The New York Times Magazine*, August 11, 1974, p. 24.

2. Ibid., p. 16.

3. Colette Dowling, "The Song of Toni Morrison," *The New York Times Magazine*, May 20, 1979, p. 54.

4. Ibid.

5. Thomas LeClair, "'The Language Must Not Sweat,'" *New Republic*, March 21, 1981, p. 27.

6. Karen De Witt, "Toni Morrison's Saga of a Black Family Is Being Hailed in All the Proper Places," *Washington Post*, September 30, 1977, p. C3.

7. Paula Giddings, "The Triumphant Song of Toni Morrison," *Encore American & Worldwide News*, December 12, 1977, p. 30.

8. Ibid.

9. Ibid., p. 26.

10. Ibid., pp. 26–27.

11. Jean Strouse, "Toni Morrison's Black Magic," *Newsweek*, March 30, 1981, p. 57.

12. Ibid.

13. Toni Morrison, *Song of Solomon* (New York: Knopf, 1977), unnumbered front pages.

14. "Toni Morrison: O-o-o-ooh She 'Done Fly' into the Literary Top Rank with *Song of Solomon*," *People Weekly*, January 2, 1978, p. 84.

15. Margo Jefferson, "Black Gold," *Newsweek*, September 12, 1977, p. 93.

16. Giddings, p. 27.

17. De Witt, p. C1.

18. Giddings, p. 27.

19. Strouse, p. 57.

20. Giddings, p. 27.

Chapter 7

1. Edwin McDowell, "Behind the Best Sellers: Toni Morrison," *The New York Times Book Review*, July 5, 1981, p. 18.

2. Claudia Tate, ed., *Black Women Writers at Work* (New York: Continuum, 1983), p. 120.

3. Jean Strouse, "Toni Morrison's Black Magic," *Newsweek*, March 30, 1981, p. 57.

4. Ibid.

5. Mel Watkins, "Talk with Toni Morrison," *The New York Times Book Review*, September 11, 1977, p. 50.

6. Nellie McKay, "An Interview With Toni Morrison," *Contemporary Literature*, Winter 1983, p. 417.

7. Judith Wilson, "A Conversation With Toni Morrison," *Essence*, July 1981, p. 130.

8. Janet Wiehe, "Reviews," *Library Journal*, February 15, 1981, p. 472.

9. Strouse, p. 52.

10. John Irving, "Morrison's Black Fable," *The New York Times Book Review*, March 29, 1981, p. 1.

11. Wilson, p. 130.

12. McDowell, p. 18.

13. Strouse, p. 52.

14. Dana Micucci, "An Inspired Life: Toni Morrison Writes and a Generation Listens," *Chicago Tribune*, May 31, 1992, sec. 6, p. 3.

15. Betty Fussell, "All That Jazz," *Lear's*, October 1992, p. 69.

16. Colette Dowling, "The Song of Toni Morrison," *The New York Times Magazine*, May 20, 1979, p. 42.

17. Ibid., p. 56.

18. Margaret Croyden, "Toni Morrison Tries Her Hand at Playwriting," *The New York Times*, December 29, 1985, p. H6.

19. Dardis McNamee, "Toni Morrison," *Capital Region*, January 1986, p. 32.

20. Ibid., p. 34.

21. Ibid.

22. Croyden, p. H6.

23. Ibid.

Chapter 8

1. Bonnie Angelo, "The Pain of Being Black," *Time*, May 22, 1989, p. 120.

2. Miriam Horn, "'Five Years of Terror,'" *U.S. News & World Report*, October 19, 1987, p. 75.

3. Ibid.

4. Ibid.

5. Walter Clemons, "The Ghosts of 'Sixty Million and More,'" *Newsweek*, September 28, 1987, p. 75.

6. Angelo, p. 121.

7. Ibid.

8. Claudia Dreifus, "Chloe Wofford Talks About Toni Morrison," *The New York Times Magazine*, September 11, 1994, p. 75.

9. Horn, p. 75.

10. Middleton Harris, et al., *The Black Book* (New York: Random House, 1974), p. 10.

11. Amanda Smith, "Toni Morrison," *Publishers Weekly*, August 21, 1987, p. 51.

12. Clemons, p. 75.

13. Toni Morrison, *Beloved* (New York: Knopf, 1987), dedication page.

14. Angelo, p. 120.

15. Diane Turbide, "Taking the A Train," *Maclean's*, June 1, 1992, p. 51.

16. Walter Clemons, "A Gravestone of Memories," *Newsweek*, September 28, 1987, p. 75.

17. Margaret Atwood, "Haunted by Their Nightmares," *The New York Times Book Review*, September 13, 1987, p. 1.

18. Hope Hale Davis, "Casting a Strong Spell," *The New York Leader*, November 2, 1987, p. 20.

19. Carol E. Rinzler, "For Whom the Blurbs Toll, the Most Likely to Be Talked About This Month," *Vogue*, September 1987, p. 476.

20. Robert Allen, et al., "Black Writers in Praise of Toni Morrison," *The New York Times Book Review*, January 24, 1988, p. 36.

21. Dana Micucci, "An Inspired Life: Toni Morrison Writes and a Generation Listens," *Chicago Tribune*, May 31, 1992, sec. 6, p. 3.

Chapter 9

1. Pat Emory, "Toni Morrison: Writing For and About Blacks," *Baltimore Sun*, April 5, 1987, p. 9G.

2. Liz Cobbs, "Toni Morrison Took 5 or 6 Years to Write Her First Book 'Because It Was So Much Fun,'" *Ann Arbor News*, August 8, 1990.

3. Toni Morrison, *Jazz* (New York: Knopf, 1992), p. 3.

4. Ibid., p. 4.

5. Ibid., p. 59.

6. Ibid., p. 58.

7. Andrea Stuart, "Blue Notes," *New Statesman & Society*, May 1, 1992, p. 39.

8. Nellie McKay, "An Interview with Toni Morrison," *Contemporary Literature*, Winter 1983, p. 429.

9. Diane Turbide, "Taking the A Train," *Maclean's*, June 1, 1992, p. 51.

10. Jane Smiley, "Vogue Arts—Books," *Vogue*, May 1992, p. 160.

11. Dana Micucci, "An Inspired Life: Toni Morrison Writes and a Generation Listens," *Chicago Tribune*, May 31, 1992, sec. 6, p. 3.

12. Claudia Dreifus, "Chloe Wofford Talks About Toni Morrison," *The New York Times Magazine*, September 11, 1994, p. 73.

13. Ibid., p. 74.

14. Ibid., p. 73.

Chapter 10

1. Claudia Tate, ed., *Black Women Writers at Work* (New York: Continuum, 1983), p. 131.

2. Elsie B. Washington, "Toni Morrison Now," *Essence*, October 1987, p. 137.

3. Elaine Showalter, ed., *Modern American Women Writers* (New York: Scribner, 1991), p. 317.

FURTHER READING

Harris, Laurie Lanzen, ed. *Biography Today 1994 Annual Cumulation*. Detroit: Omnigraphics, 1995, 230–239.

Morrison, Toni. *Beloved: A Novel*. New York: Knopf, 1987.

——. *The Bluest Eye*. New York: Knopf, 1970.

——. *Jazz*. New York: Knopf, 1992.

——. *Playing in the Dark: Whiteness and the Literary Imagination*. Cambridge, Mass.: Harvard University Press, 1992.

——. *Song of Solomon*. New York: Knopf, 1977.

——. *Sula*. New York: Knopf, 1973.

——. *Tar Baby*. New York: Knopf, 1981.

Showalter, Elaine, ed. *Modern American Women Writers*. New York: Scribner, 1991, 317–338.

Smith, Jessie Carney, ed. *Epic Lives: One Hundred Black Women Who Made a Difference*. Detroit: Visible Ink Press, 1993, 380–386.

Smith, Valerie, ed. *African American Writers*. New York: Scribner, 1991, 321–333.

Taylor-Guthrie, Danille, ed. *Conversations With Toni Morrison*. Jackson: University Press of Mississippi, 1994.

INDEX

A

Ali, Muhammad, 46
Angelo, Bonnie (*Time*), 76
Atwood, Margaret (*The New
    York Times Book Review*), 77
Austen, Jane, 20

B

Bambara, Toni Cade, 46
Black Book, The, 46-48, 73
Blackburn, Sara (*The New York
    Times*), 43
Brown v. *Board of Education of
    Topeka*, 25
Bryant, Jerry H. (*The Nation*), 44

C

Cather, Willa, 20, 88
Cavett, Dick, 62
Civil War, 16, 74, 77
Clemons, Walter (*Newsweek*), 77
Cornell University, 22, 25
Croyden, Margaret (*The New
    York Times*), 68

D

Davis, Angela, 46
Davis, Hope Hale (*The New
    Leader*), 77
Dowling, Collette (*The New
    York Times*), 28, 63
Dreifus, Claudia (*The New York
    Times Magazine*), 92
Dumas, Henry, 46

E

Emancipation Proclamation, 17

F

Faulkner, William, 20
Fitzgerald, F. Scott, 84
Frankel, Haskel (*The New York
    Times Book Review*), 37
Fugitive Slave Bill, 73
Furman, Roger, 47
Fussell, Betty (*Lear's*), 62

G

Garner, Margaret, 73-74
Goheen, Robert F., 82

H

Harris, Middleton A. (Spike), 47
Harvard University, 87
Hawthorne, Nathaniel, 21
Hemingway, Ernest, 20, 88
Hill, Anita, 88-89
Holocaust, 77-78
Howard University, 20-22,
    25-28, 94
Howard University Players, 22
Hurston, Zora Neale, 56

I

Irving, John (*The New York
    Times Book Review*), 61

J

Jefferson, Margo (*Newsweek*),
    53-54

Jones, Gayl, 46

K

King Carl XVI Gustaf, 91
King, Martin Luther, Jr., 68

L

Lee, Spike, 97
Levitt, Morris, 47
Lorain, Ohio, 12, 28-29, 31-32,
    55, 93
Lorain Public Library, 93

M

Matrix Awards, 93-94
Melville, Herman, 21
Micucci, Dana (*Chicago
    Tribune*), 62
Morrison, Harold (husband), 25,
    28
Morrison, Harold Ford (son),
    25, 43, 48, 55, 90
Morrison, Slade Kevin (son), 28,
    43, 48, 55, 90
Morrison, Toni
    ancestors, 12, 14-18, 50
    as Chloe Anthony Wofford,
        12-21, 35
    books of
        Beloved: A Novel, 11,
            69-81, 89, 96
        Bluest Eye, The, 11, 27-38
        Jazz, 11, 82-87, 88, 89
        *Playing in the Dark:
            Whiteness and the
            Literary Imagination*,
            87-88
        Race-ing Justice,

*En-Gendering Power:
    Essays on Anita
    Hill, Clarence
    Thomas, and the
    Construction of Social
    Reality*, 88-89
    Song of Solomon, 11,
        48-55, 89
    Sula, 11, 38-46, 97
    Tar Baby, 11, 56-62, 97
    childhood, 12-20
    college, 20-25
    editing, 11, 29-31, 39,
        45-48, 53, 55, 63
    marriage and divorce, 25,
        28, 63
    motherhood, 25, 28-29,
        39-40, 42-43, 48,
        50-53
    on criticism of her work,
        35, 37, 44-45, 61
    on success, 54-55, 80, 90,
        96
    on writing, 11, 29, 31-37,
        40, 52-53, 56-57, 67,
        94, 96
    play, *Dreaming Emmett*,
        63-68
    siblings, 12-13, 55, 89
    teaching, 11, 25, 28,
        38-39, 48, 63, 81-82
Moses, Gilbert, 67-68

N

National Book Award, 45, 78
National Book Critics Circle
    Award, 54, 78

Nobel, Alfred, 8
Nobel Prize in literature, 7-11, 89-90

P
Parks, Rosa, 67
Poe, Edgar Allan, 88
Princeton University, 7, 82
Pulitzer Prize, 11, 80

R
Rinzler, Carol E. (*Vogue*), 78
Roosevelt, Franklin D., 14

S
Shakespeare, William, 21
Smiley, Jane (*Vogue*), 87
Smith, Ernest, 47
State University of New York at Albany, 63, 82
State University of New York at Purchase, 38
Strouse, Jean (*Newsweek*), 60-61
Stuart, Andrea (*New Statesman & Society*), 87

T
Tallchief, Maria, 11

Temple, Shirley, 34-35
Texas Southern University, 25
Thomas, Clarence, 88-89
Till, Emmett, 65, 67
Turbide, Diane (*Maclean's*), 87
Twain, Mark, 88

V
Van der Zee, James, 84

W
Wiehe, Janet (*Library Journal*), 60
Winfrey, Oprah, 96
Wofford, George (father), 12-14, 18, 52-53, 55
Wofford, Ramah (mother), 12, 14-15, 55, 89
Wright, Richard, 54

Y
Yale University, 48
Young, Andrew, 46